Kids Know
DINOSAURS

VICTOR IMOMOH

DEDICATION

This book is part of a series dedicated to my kids: Ethan, Victoria, and Ian, who constantly were an inspiration to writing the entire series. They encouraged me, from start to completion, to see that the book gets published for sale on Amazon.

CONTENTS

ACKNOWLEDGEMENT

Special thanks to all the children who inspired me to
write this book. Your curiosity, enthusiasm, and joy for
learning are what make writing for kids so much fun. I
hope this book brings you as much joy and wonder as
you bring to the world every day. Keep exploring,
imagining, and dreaming big

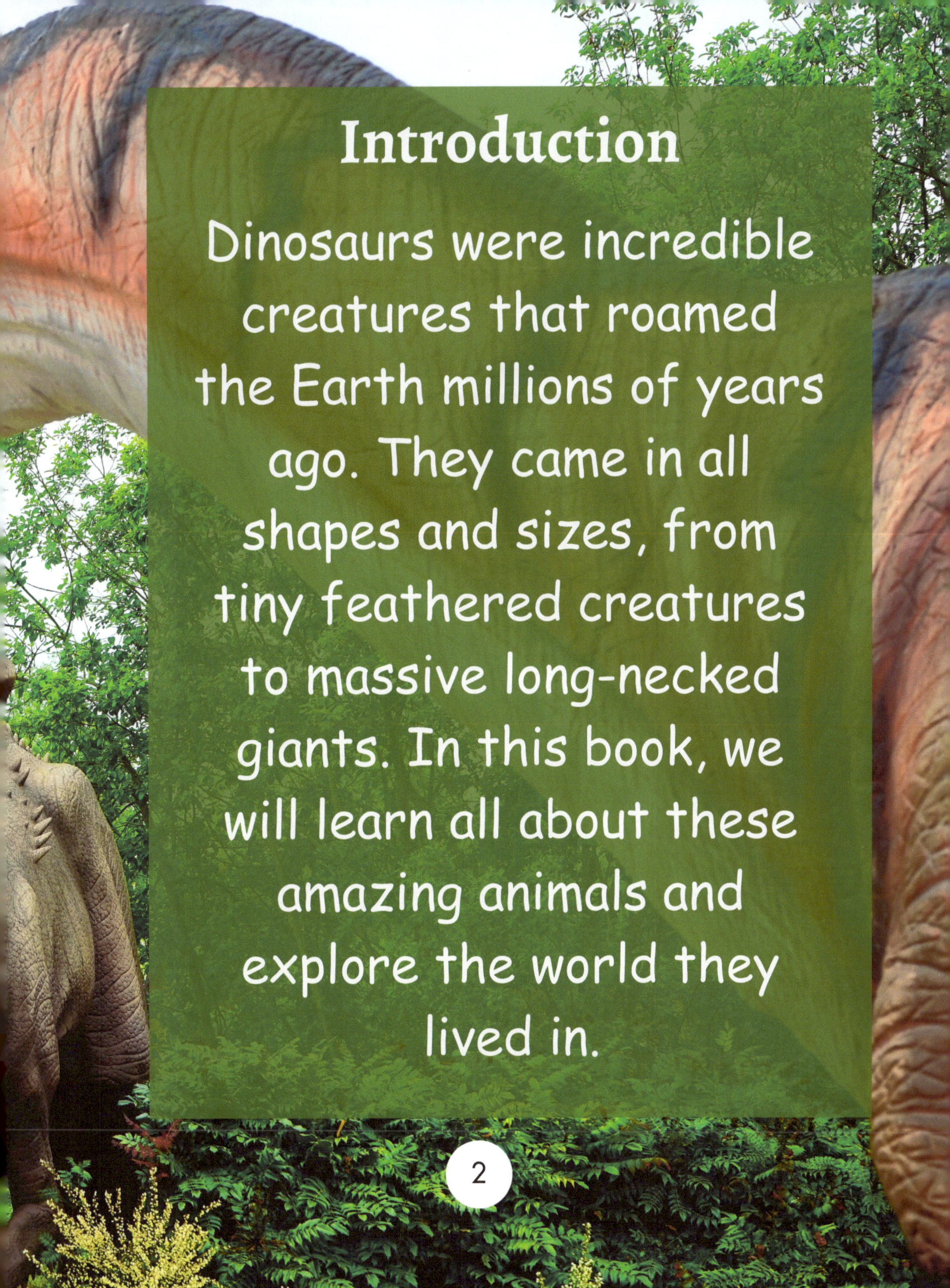

Introduction

Dinosaurs were incredible creatures that roamed the Earth millions of years ago. They came in all shapes and sizes, from tiny feathered creatures to massive long-necked giants. In this book, we will learn all about these amazing animals and explore the world they lived in.

Tyrannosaurus Rex

Chapter 1: What are Dinosaurs?

Dinosaurs are a group of reptiles that lived millions of years ago and are known for their unique skeletal structures, including their long necks and tails, and their bipedal* stance. There were two main groups of dinosaurs: the Saurischia, which had a pelvis similar to that of modern

*Bipedal means being able to walk on two hinge legs

lizards and birds, and the Ornithischia, which had a pelvis more like that of modern mammals. Within these groups, there were many different types of dinosaurs, each with their own unique characteristics and adaptations, such as the giant sauropods, the speedy theropods, and the armored ankylosaurs.

An Ankylosaur

Example of Ornithischiau

A Sauropod

A Theropod

Chapter 2: Age of Dinosaurs

The Mesozoic Era was divided into three periods: Triassic, Jurassic, and Cretaceous. Warm and moist conditions with abundant vegetation provided ideal habitats for dinosaurs to evolve and dominate the terrestrial ecosystem for over 160 million years.

Chapter 3: Feathers and Scales

Dinosaurs had varied skin coverings, ranging from scales to feathers. Recent research suggests feathers evolved from simple hair-like structures, with famous feathered dinosaurs like Velociraptor, Archaeopteryx, and the four-winged Microraptor showcasing their plumage.

Stegosaurus

Iguanodon

Chapter 4: Nesting and Herding

Herbivorous and carnivorous dinosaurs were studied by paleontologists through fossilized evidence to infer their behavior. Nesting and herding behaviors have been observed in fossilized dinosaurs like Maiasaura, hadrosaurs, and theropods such as Allosaurus.

Chapter 5: Eggs and Babies

Dinosaurs laid eggs in nests with a variety of shapes and sizes. The eggs hatched after incubation, and the babies grew quickly. Some dinosaurs went through a bipedal phase before becoming fully grown adults, while others had different stages of growth depending on their species.

A Velociraptor

Credit: Natural History Museum, USA.

Chapter 6: Discovering Dinosaurs

Dinosaur discovery dates back to the 19th century, with famous fossils like Tyrannosaurus rex and Triceratops being found in North America. Scientists such as Mary Anning and Robert Bakker have contributed significantly to our understanding of these prehistoric creatures.

Chapter 7: Dinosaur Fossils

Dinosaur fossils form when remains are buried in sediment and mineralized over time. Fossil types include bones, teeth, eggs, and footprints. They reveal prehistoric life and evolution, informing our understanding of Earth's history.

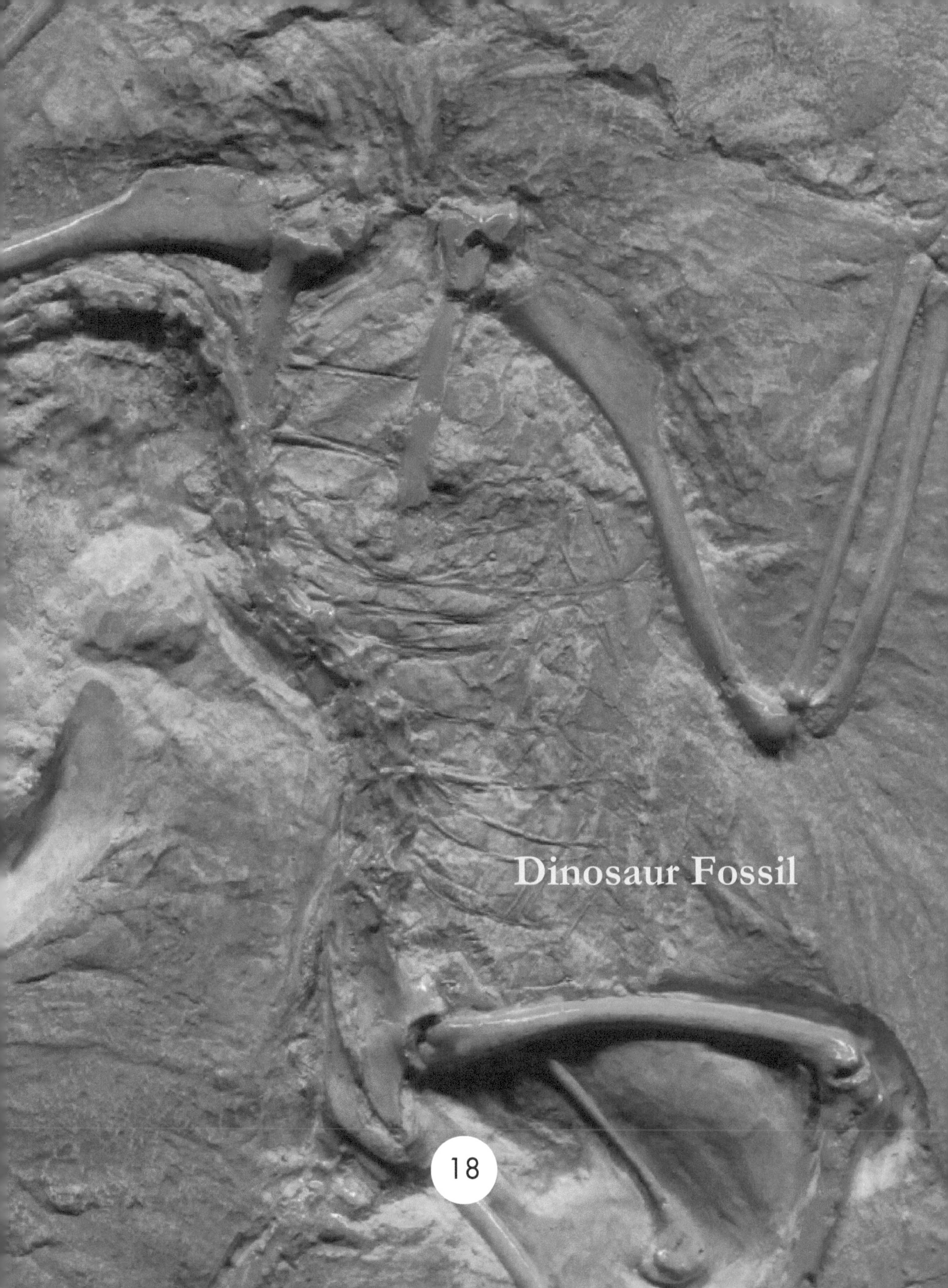
Dinosaur Fossil

Chapter 8: Parks and Museums

Dinosaur parks and museums are popular attractions worldwide, showcasing fossils and exhibits. The American Museum of Natural History and Royal Tyrrell Museum are famous.

T-REX
They offer educational programs, interactive exhibits, and paleontological (ancient biological studies) research opportunities.

A Titanosaur

Chapter 9: Dinosaur Fun Facts

Fun facts about dinosaurs: the longest was over 100 foot Argentinosaurus; the heaviest was the 100-ton Argentinosaurus; the smallest was the 2-pound Anchiornis; and some dinosaurs had feathers, not scales.

Chapter 10: Conclusion

Dinosaurs have captivated and inspired people of all ages in art, pop culture, and science. Whether through museums, movies, or fossil digs, the fascination with dinosaurs persists. So let's continue to learn and explore, and keep their legacy alive for generations to come.

24

Credit: A World of Dinosaurs, 2019. TIME for Kids.

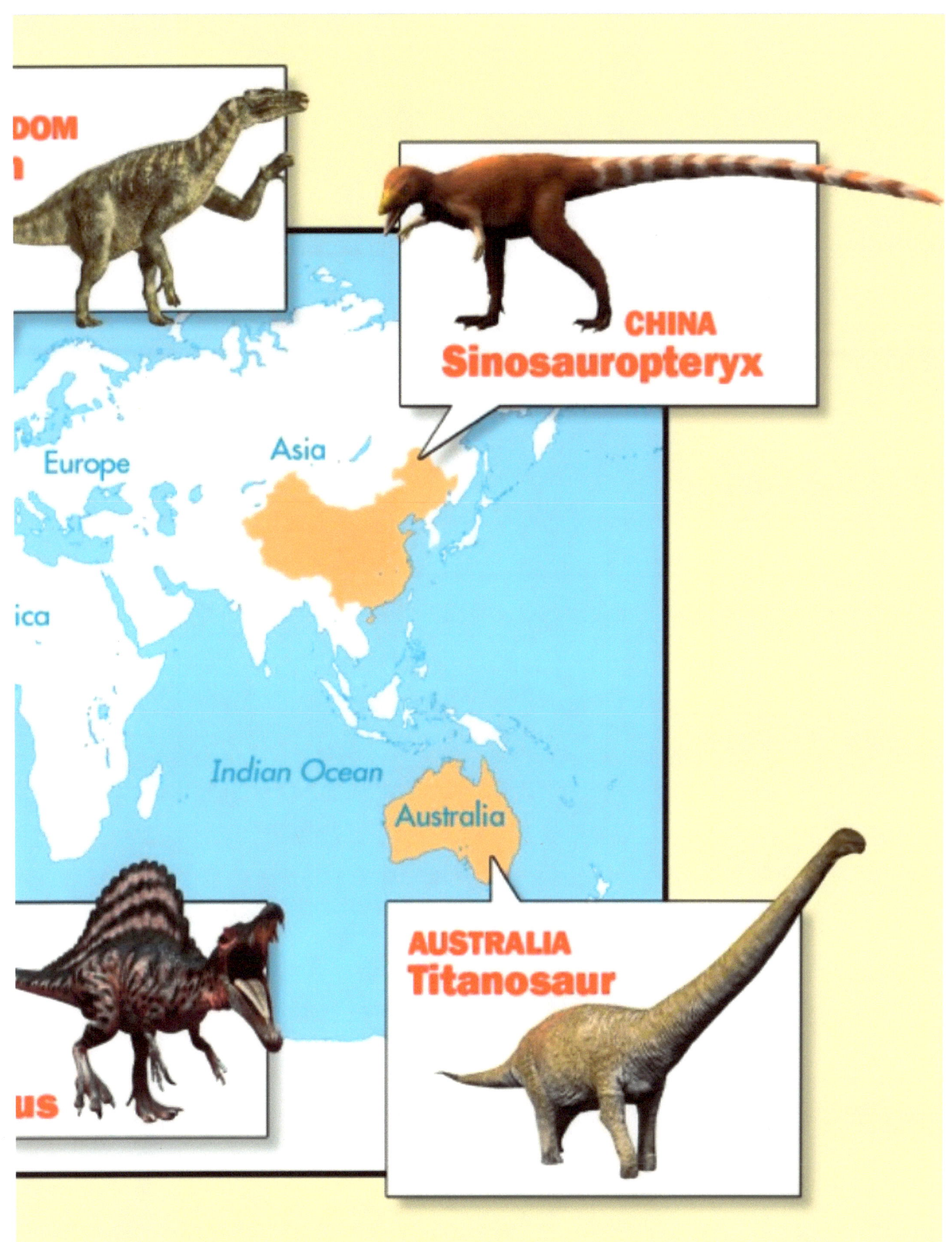
DOM
CHINA
Sinosauropteryx
Europe
Asia
Indian Ocean
Australia
AUSTRALIA
Titanosaur
us